50 Brilliant PE Challenges
Using Just a
Beanbag

Will Hussey

We hope you and your pupils enjoy using the ideas in this book. Listed below are a few of our other books which might be of interest to you. Information on these and all our other books can be found on our website: www.brilliantpublications.co.uk.

Other books in the series
50 Brilliant PE Challenges Using Just a Hoop
50 Brilliant PE Challenges Using Just a Tennis Ball

Other PE books
100+ Fun Ideas for Teaching PE Games
43 Team-building Activities for KS1
43 Team-building Activities for KS1
100+ Fun Ideas for Playground Games

Other books written by Will Hussey
Where Can an Elephant Hide?
Where Can an Elephant Roost?
Brilliant Activities to Stimulate Creative Thinking

Published by Brilliant Publications
Unit 10
Sparrow Hall Farm
Edlesborough
Dunstable
Bedfordshire
LU6 2ES, UK

www.brilliantpublications.co.uk

The name Brilliant Publications and the logo are registered trademarks.

Written by Will Hussey
Illustrations and cover illustration by Chantel Ke

© Text Will Hussey 2014
© Design Brilliant Publications 2014
ISBN printed book: 978-1-78317-140-8
ISBN e-pdf: 978–1-78317-144-6

First printed and published in the UK in 2015

The right of Will Hussey to be identified as the author of this work has been asserted by herself in accordance with the Copyright, Designs and Patents Act 1988.

No part of this book may be reproduced in any other form or for any other purpose without the prior permission of the publisher.

Contents

Introduction 4

Individual challenges
1. Sitting duck 1 5
2. Hurricane 6
3. Elbow pad 7
4. Headstrong 8
5. Body shot 9
6. Back flick 10
7. Flick back 11
8. Toe to toe 12
9. Double decker 13

Group/pair challenges
10. Has bean 14
11. Headway 15
12. Pancake 16
13. Hip hop 17
14. Turtle 18
15. Bottoms up 19
16. Morph 20
17. Fetch 21
18. Hopscotch 22
19. Hot potato beans 23
20. Volley 24
21. Cast-off 25
22. Bean work 26
23. Bag to back 27
24. Scarecrow 28
25. Make beans 29

26. Downfall 30
27. Bag transfer 31
28. Spill the beans 32
29. Leap pad 33
30. Bean badger 34
31. Welly beans 35
32. Beanstalk 36

Class challenges
33. Harvest 37
34. Sitting duck 2 38
35. Burial bag 39
36. Travel bag 40
37. Last bag standing 41
38. Jelly bean 42
39. Jumping bean 43
40. Interval 44
41. Extinguish 45
42. Elbow grease 46
43. Trampoline 47
44. Straight ahead 48
45. Bean and gone 49
46. Throw back 50
47. Bean stack 51
48. Rainbow 52
49. Smuggle 53
50. Recruit 54

Index (by level of difficulty) ... 55

50 Brilliant PE Challenges Using Just a Beanbag

Introduction

50 Brilliant PE Challenges Using Just a Beanbag does exactly what it says on the tin.

This handy teacher resource will provide a wealth of active and enjoyable activities, inspiring outstanding learning with minimal preparation.

A mixture of differentiated individual, group and whole class activities, with suggestions for further challenge and extension, ensures the busy teacher can create bespoke lessons.

The **50 Brilliant PE Challenges** series of books believes less is more: inclusive competition and engagement facilitated by minimal preparation and resources regardless of subject expertise. Brilliant challenges create brilliant PE lessons!

Key

👤	Individual challenge
👥	Group/paired challenge
👨‍👩‍👧‍👦	Whole class challenge
☆	Moderate difficulty
☆☆	Intermediate
☆☆☆	Advanced

1. Sitting duck 1

Challenge

Participants try to cover a stipulated distance with a minimum number of throws. Each throw must be executed whilst sitting cross-legged. Only when the beanbag has landed, can the pupil move to sit in the new position and throw again.

Tip
Despite throwing from a sitting position, it is still possible to use the upper body to generate extra power and distance.

Development
Players may challenge each other to be the first to clear an agreed distance. The beanbag should not be thrown until an individual is sat firmly on the ground.

2. Hurricane

Challenge

Compete to see who can throw a beanbag the furthest, with a discus-style throw. The child must complete a 360° rotation before hurling the beanbag.

Tip
Release the beanbag when the throwing arm is pointing approximately 45° in the direction of throw.

Development
Using the other hand, and therefore completing a rotation in the opposite direction, often requires significant adjustment.

3. Elbow pad

Challenge

Rest a beanbag just above the elbow of a bent arm, and in one swift movement attempt to straighten the arm, catching the beanbag in the process.

Tip
The success of this activity relies on speed; bring the hand to grasp the beanbag before gravity has time to take effect!

Development
Children who are initially successful relish the challenge to see how many beanbags they can catch in the same way. Try balancing two, then three and so on …

4. Headstrong

Challenge
Aim to stack as many beanbags as possible on top of the head without one falling off.

Tip
Flatten the beanbags evenly before positioning them to aid stability. Children may choose to work with a friend, assisting each other with placing the beanbags in to position.

Development
Try to travel a short distance whilst balancing the beanbags.

5. Body shot

Challenge
Participants try to throw and catch a beanbag on as many different parts of their body as possible.

Tip
Throwing the beanbag accurately with as little force as possible makes it easier to 'cushion' and catch it.

Development:
How high can you throw the beanbag whilst still managing to catch it successfully?

6. Back flick

Challenge
Place the beanbag on the back of your heel and stand as though you are about to begin hopping. Flick your foot in order to send the beanbag over your head before endeavouring to catch it in front with both hands.

Tip
Position hands with fingers splayed before flicking the beanbag to maximise chances of catching.

Development
Can the beanbag be successfully flicked and caught off both legs? How many consecutive catches can be achieved?

7. Flick back

Challenge

The reverse of **Back flick**, participants should endeavour to flip the beanbag backwards over their head and attempt to catch it on the back of one raised heel.

Tip
Try to throw the beanbag so that it falls vertically, whilst retaining an upright body position.

Development
Once the beanbag has been caught using both legs, cooperate with a friend by asking them to throw the beanbag.

8. Toe to toe

Challenge

Having mastered the previous challenges, encourage participants to flick a beanbag with their foot overhead to catch with a raised heel.

Development
Try this activity in reverse; flicking the beanbag from behind to catch in front on an extended foot.

9. Double decker

Challenge

How far can you throw two beanbags consecutively so that the second rests directly on top of the first?

Tip
Start by dropping both beanbags directly in front of you and then, incrementally, extend the distance.

Development
Try using three beanbags instead of two or, alternatively collaborate with a friend to take a throw each.

50 Brilliant PE Challenges Using Just a Beanbag

10. Has bean

Challenge
Participants make their way along a series of coloured beanbags, trying to memorise the order the colours are arranged in. They should then relay the order by memory to a friend, who checks for accuracy. Swap roles.

Tip
Suggest that the children walk along the sequence of beanbags without stopping.

Development
Can the children relay the order of beanbags in reverse?

11. Headway

> Groups of children race against each other whilst balancing a beanbag on top of their heads. **Challenge**

Tip
Insist that anyone who drops the beanbag must replace it and retreat three paces before continuing.

Development
Of course balancing two beanbags on top of their head is more challenging than one or competing relay fashion as a member of a team.

12. Pancake

Challenge

Participants race against each other to reach the finish line, balancing a beanbag on the back of an outstretched hand.

Tip
Splaying the fingers creates a larger area on which to balance the beanbag.

Development
Suggest that the children should 'toss' the beanbag as they proceed; flipping it over from one side to the other.

13. Hip hop

Challenge

Participants race against each other by hopping on one leg with a beanbag secured in the crook of their other knee. Should a competitor overbalance or drop the beanbag they must return to the start.

Tip
Looking straight ahead and avoiding the tendency to look down helps children to concentrate on maintaining balance.

Development
Try the same activity with two or even more beanbags.

14. Turtle

Challenge
Relay teams compete to see who can be the first to transport a beanbag balanced on their back, around a course, moving on all fours.

Tip
Place the beanbag in the small of the back to help minimise the possibility of it slipping off.

Development
Suggest participants must also secure a beanbag between their feet thus requiring them to further adapt their technique.

15. Bottoms up

Pairs of children stand back to back and try to pass the beanbag above their heads and through their legs alternately.

Challenge

Tip
Position the feet shoulder-width apart and try not to lean back against your partner.

Development
See which partnership can achieve the most number of passes in a given time limit.

16. Morph

Challenge
A group of four children begin with approximately 12 beanbags. The opposing team chooses a number from 1 to 9, which the first group must then try to form on the ground by placing beanbags one at a time in relay fashion. The other team take turns individually to see how many times they can circle the pattern before it is completed. Both teams then swap over to try and beat the existing total.

Tip
Stipulate that there must be at least two large paces between the pile of beanbags and the pattern.

Development
Increase or decrease the number of participants or beanbags used.

17. Fetch

Challenge

Two teams compete to collect the most red beanbags, which are hidden under piles of other beanbags. Participants take turns to remove one beanbag at a time from any of the piles, making the red beanbags accessible (red beanbags can only be retrieved when they are completely uncovered.) The game finishes when all the red beanbags have been collected.

Tip
A beanbag can also be replaced on a pile, thwarting another group's chance to retrieve a red one that has just become 'available'.

Development
Apportion points values to beanbags of different colours.

18. Hopscotch

Challenge
Children take it in turns to attempt a hopscotch course, hopping and jumping upon pre-positioned beanbags. Each time the whole of the team successfully completes the course, an additional hop and jump footprint is added.

Tip
Flatten the beanbags to make them easier to step on. Position appropriate to the team member with the shortest stride.

Development
Create alternative patterns and pathways, encouraging the children to change direction and complete consecutive hops and jumps.

19. Hot potato beans

Challenge
Six children form a circle and throw a beanbag to anyone within that circle. Should they take longer than three seconds or drop the beanbag or be the cause of a misthrow, they should lose a life and sink to one knee. A second mistake results in their exclusion from the game.

Tip
Ensure that the children are evenly spaced, and stipulate that they must remain in position without straying in to other player's territory.

Development
Increase the gaps between players and/or suggest children are only allowed to use one hand – and then the other hand.

20. Volley

Challenge
Partners collaborate to see how far one can flip a beanbag with their foot towards the other who in turn endeavours to catch it.

Tip
Start gradually, standing approximately three paces apart. Take an extra step back with each successful catch.

Development
Ensure each child takes a turn at sending and receiving the beanbag, using different feet and either hand to flip and catch respectively.

21. Cast-off

Challenge

Children race to complete a course hindered by balancing a beanbag upon one foot. If the beanbag touches the ground they must return to the start.

Tip
Maintaining a walking action where both feet touch the ground alternately often proves effective, creating a smooth continuous action least likely to dislodge the beanbag.

Development
Suggest the children swap the beanbag to their other foot before embarking upon a return leg.

50 Brilliant PE Challenges Using Just a Beanbag

22. Bean work

Pairs of children collaborate to transport a beanbag by sandwiching it in between their adjoining feet.

Tip
Partners of comparable height are best suited to this task, enabling steps of similar length.

Development
Try linking three participants in similar fashion to transport two beanbags, or create an even longer chain.

23. Bag to back

Challenge

Collaborating partners aim to stand from a seated cross-legged position, ensuring a beanbag remains sandwiched between their backs in the process. Participants are not allowed to touch the ground with their hands.

Tip
Some participants choose to link arms, which may help depending upon the positioning of the beanbag.

Development
How many successful partnerships can children form with their classmates?

24. Scarecrow

> **Challenge**
> One child stands with arms outstretched. A partner piles as many beanbags as possible on top. How many beanbags they can transport in this way without losing any?

Tip
The player transporting the beanbags should turn their palms skywards; this usually seems to be the most successful method.

Development
Teams of children compete with each other in relay fashion to see how many beanbags can be transported within a particular time limit. If a beanbag is dropped it cannot be picked up again.

25. Make beans

> **Challenge**
> Two teams of five children compete to score the most goals. Each team selects a player who must stand in position, ready to catch a beanbag thrown towards them. Teams must complete three consecutive passes before attempting to 'score' in this way. No moving/travelling with the beanbag is allowed.

Tip
Situate opposing goal-catchers at opposite ends of the playing area.

Development
Suggest children must complete a greater number of passes before scoring; introduce a time limit for how long a player can hold onto the beanbag, or increase/decrease the number of players on each team.

26. Downfall

Challenge
Children compete to see how many individuals can catch a beanbag from a cluster thrown by one member of the group. Launch the same number of beanbags as participants.

Tip
Players should organise themselves in a semi-circle around the person throwing the beanbags.

Development
Rotate the participants throwing the beanbags, and accumulate points for every beanbag caught. Compare scores with other groups.

27. Bag transfer

Challenge

Pairs of children begin by facing each other, each with a beanbag balanced upon one foot. On an agreed signal, they simultaneously flick their beanbag towards each other, whilst attempting to catch the incoming beanbag with their hand.

Tip
Attempt to flick the beanbag in a slightly higher trajectory than directly to your partner; this will generate additional time to prepare for the catch.

Development
Suggest children try balancing the beanbag on either foot. Extending the distance between pairs makes the challenge more tricky. Harder still, balance a beanbag on both feet, necessitating a nifty 'double,' kick.

28. Spill the beans

Challenge

A pair of children work together to see how many beanbags one of them can catch and retain before dropping one. One child throws the beanbags from an agreed distance to their partner, and continues passing them one at a time until the point of overload is reached.

Tip
The player receiving the beanbags can re-arrange them before receiving the next pass, creating a target area for their partner.

Development
Increase the distance over which the beanbags are thrown. Insist that the player who has caught the beanbags must then try to return them after acquiring a certain number (similarly without dropping one.)

29. Leap pad

Challenge
Teams of four children compete against each other to negotiate a 'swamp' by creating stepping-stone platforms from sixteen beanbags. If a team member steps into the swamp, the team must return to the start line.

Tip
Create platforms sufficiently large for a foot to be placed upon them.

Development
Reduce the number of beanbags available for a team to use. Introduce additional beanbags that each team member must balance upon their head throughout.

30. Bean badger

Challenge

One child stands with their eyes closed and hands outstretched preparing to receive a beanbag. A partner stands five paces away and attempts to throw three beanbags in succession, aiming at the target presented.

Tip
Turn palms upwards and ensure hands are touching with fingers spread wide, maximising the target area.

Development
Increase the distance between partners.

31. Welly beans

Challenge
Pairs of children attempt to throw a beanbag over the maximum possible distance, keeping the throwing arm straight as if 'wanging' a wellington boot. The throw is only deemed successful if the beanbag is caught.

Tip
Start with shorter more manageable distances and increase gradually.

Development
Try using both arms to 'wang' the beanbag.

32. Beanstalk

Challenge

A child takes aim at their partner, attempting to land a beanbag upon the top of their head. They must then try to throw the beanbag through the hole created by an arm when saluting. Do this with both arms. Beanbags must be thrown underarm with care.

Tip
Begin by standing only a couple of steps apart, moving further away with greater confidence and success.

Development
Introduce an extra person as an additional target; either stood adjacent to the first or directly behind.

33. Harvest

Challenge

The class is divided in to teams, who compete in relay fashion to collect the most beanbags. Red beanbags are worth double.

Tip
Ensure the red beanbags are evenly scattered. Consider changing the value of the beanbags between rounds.

Development
Scatter the beanbags over a wider area. Insist children run in pairs, linking hands until they return to their teams.

34. Sitting duck 2

Challenge

Several children are chosen to be 'on'. They attempt to chase and tag the other competitors. There are 10 beanbags positioned around the playing area which individuals may sit on cross-legged to gain temporary sanctuary from pursuers.

Tip
A child who has been tagged is not allowed to 'tag-back,' the person who has just caught them.

Development
Increase the number of players who are 'on,' or vary the number of beanbags that can be used as sanctuary.

35. Burial bag

> **Challenge**
> The children are allocated teams, who simultaneously attempt to recover 30 beanbags that have been 'hidden,' prior to the start of the game. The winning team is the one that manages to collect the most beanbags.

Tip
Every beanbag that is discovered must be returned to the team's starting point before the finder may continue searching.

Development
Award red beanbags 'double points' status; stipulate beanbags must be retrieved in a particular colour order or suggest participants must search in pairs.

36. Travel bag

Challenge
Teams compete to be the first to complete a course. The first person runs to a pile of beanbags, collecting one and returning to the rest of the team. The first and second person then complete the course together, jointly holding the beanbag and collecting a second along the way. The chain gets longer until the whole team have navigated the course in this manner.

Tip
Teams should adjust their pace with consideration for the first member of the team, who has the furthest to run.

Development
Create a more complex course to negotiate or increase the number of competitors in each team.

37. Last bag standing

Challenge

Every player begins the game with a beanbag. Each child attempts to throw their beanbag at any of the other participants endeavouring to hit them below the knee, rendering that player out of the game. The last player to remain in the game is the winner.

Tip
Children are allowed to try and avoid the throws of other players, but 'blocking,' the beanbag is not permitted.

Development
Some children start the game without a beanbag, whilst others can be armed with more than one.

38. Jelly bean

Challenge
Four children begin the game with a beanbag, each with a different colour. They attempt to build a team by throwing their beanbags and hitting other participants below the knee. The person who has been hit collects a beanbag of the same colour as the one they were targeted with, before trying to catch other players in the same manner. The game finishes when everyone has been hit – the winning team is the one with the most members.

Tip
Prepare four easily accessible piles of sorted beanbags prior to commencing the game.

Development
Remove surplus beanbags of a certain colour mid-way through the game, causing an exiting player to re-enter without a beanbag until they are targeted again by an available colour.

39. Jumping bean

Challenge
Teams compete relay fashion to be the first to transport a beanbag around a course, jumping two-footed with a beanbag sandwiched between their feet.

Tip
Competitors who drop the beanbag must stop and take three paces backwards, before replacing the beanbag and continuing.

Development
Handicap some players/teams by insisting they sandwich two or more beanbags between their feet.

40. Interval

Challenge

A large oval track is demarcated by placing different-coloured beanbags at various intervals. The children jog around the track, accelerating when they reach a red beanbag until they reach the next one when they resume jogging.

Tip
Ensure the gaps after a red beanbag until the next are variable, encouraging a variety of different speeds.

Development
Extend the length of the track or distances between beanbags, or instruct the children to accelerate between beanbags of a different colour.

41. Extinguish

Challenge

Two children are selected as the 'hot-feet,' who begin with 30 beanbags piled around their feet. They attempt to clear the area of beanbags by throwing them in any direction. The rest of the class endeavour to return them before all the beanbags have been ejected.

Tip
The 'hot-feet' players must throw the beanbags underarm. Classmates returning the beanbags should place the beanbags rather than throw them.

Development
Introduce two opposing 'hot-feet' teams, each trying to deposit the beanbags thrown by the opposing team's 'hot-feet' throwers.

42. Elbow grease

Challenge
Pairs of children compete to be the first to the finish, transporting a beanbag sandwiched between their adjoining elbows. Should the beanbag fall to the ground the partnership must return to the starting point.

Tip
Placing the arm that is not being used behind the back seems to curtail the urge to travel too quickly, which inevitably leads to dropping the beanbag.

Development
Suggest that children compete in a chain of three or maybe four people.

43. Trampoline

Challenge

Half a dozen children are selected to take a beanbag. The rest of the children disperse around the playing area. Each of the chosen beanbag holders race around the rest of the class, attempting to pass their beanbag to as many different people as possible in the time allowed. Receivers must have both legs off the ground for the catch to count.

Tip
A short countdown preceding the throw often helps to enable a successful 'mid-air' catch.

Development
Each child that has completed a pass proceeds to sit down rendering them unavailable for other catches. The game has finished when all but the children in possession of beanbags are sitting down.

44. Straight ahead

Challenge
Children are divided into teams, with each member working in relay to extend a straight line of beanbags between two stipulated points, placing one at a time. The winning team is the one deemed to have created the straightest most evenly-spaced line in the time allowed.

Tip
Suggest the children agree how many paces apart to position each beanbag before beginning.

Development
Stipulate that the beanbags must be placed in a particular order of colour.

45. Bean and gone

Challenge
Each team must select a 'mule' who is responsible for transporting their team's beanbags across a divide. The mule can make multiple journeys and the remainder of the team assist with loading the beanbags. Should a beanbag drop to the floor in transition it cannot be retrieved. The winning team is the one to have transported the most in the time available.

Tip
Swap the mule for every journey made. Do not overload the mule.

Development
Suggest teams can pick up the beanbags dropped by opposing teams and add them to their own pile awaiting transport.

46. Throw back

Challenge

Divide the class into teams of four or five children. Each team competes to be the first to throw their beanbags over the finish line. Players have a beanbag each and throw simultaneously. The team must regroup by the beanbag that has achieved the shortest distance and prepare to throw again. Continue in this manner until the finish line is reached.

Tip
Any beanbags that make contact mid-throw with a player, cause the offending team to return to the start.

Development
Try throwing two handed or using the 'weaker' arm.

47. Bean stack

> **Challenge**
> All available beanbags are scattered around the playing area. Six teams compete in relay fashion to collect beanbags one at a time, and stack them in a vertical tower. Should the tower topple over, the team is declared out of the game and the redundant beanbags can now be utilised by other teams. The winning team creates the tallest stack in the time available, or by default is the only team left.

Tip
Only the beanbag at the top of the tower can be touched.

Development
Apportion a double-points value to one colour of beanbag.

48. Rainbow

Challenge
Each team has a parallel row of six mixed-colour beanbags positioned in front of them. A further bank of beanbags lies beyond these rows. The referee declares the required colours in a specified order: red, yellow, green, blue and red, for example. Teams compete to be the first to recreate this order, by substituting the beanbags.

Tip
Team members compete in relay, taking it in turns to substitute one beanbag at a time. A player can use their go to either reject an unwanted beanbag or select a replacement – but not both.

Development
Extend the sequence of beanbags to be re-ordered. Alternatively, change the required order mid-way through the game!

49. Smuggle

Challenge

One half of the class faces away from the other half, who discretely choose a player responsible for 'smuggling,' a beanbag past the opposition. The opposing team must try to tag the carrier before they reach an agreed marker to score; if someone is mistakenly tagged who is not carrying the beanbag the perpetrator must exit the game.

Tip
Teams take alternate attempts. One person must remain solely in possession of the beanbag for each attempt.

Development
Divide the class in to three or even four teams.

50. Recruit

Challenge

Four teams each stand by a pile of beanbags of uniform colour. The rest of the class position themselves in the playing area with arms outstretched. The four teams compete to 'claim,' as many of their peers as possible in the time allowed, by placing a beanbag in their hands. The opposing players can either place a beanbag of their own on a player who is unclaimed, or remove a beanbag that has already been staked.

Tip
Competing team members can only place one beanbag at a time, or alternatively retrieve one of a competing player's beanbags at a time.

Development
Space the remainder of the class with arms outstretched over a larger area.

Index (by level of difficulty)

Moderate difficulty
1. Sitting duck 1 5
10. Has bean 14
11. Headway 15
12. Pancake 16
13. Hip hop 17
14. Turtle 18
15. Bottoms up 19
16. Morph 20
17. Fetch 21
18. Hopscotch 22
19. Hot potato beans 23
33. Harvest 37
34. Sitting duck 2 38
35. Burial bag 39
36. Travel bag 40
37. Last bag standing 41
38. Jelly bean 42
39. Jumping bean 43
40. Interval 44

Intermediate
2. Hurricane 6
3. Elbow pad 7
4. Headstrong 8
20. Volley 24
21. Cast-off 25

22. Bean work 26
23. Bag to back 27
24. Scarecrow 28
25. Make beans 29
26. Downfall 30
27. Bag transfer 31
28. Spill the beans 32
29. Leap pad 33
30. Bean badger 34
31. Welly beans 35
41. Extinguish 45
42. Elbow grease 46
43. Trampoline 47
44. Straight ahead 48
45. Bean and gone 49
46. Throw back 50
47. Bean stack 51
48. Rainbow 52

Advanced
5. Body shot 9
6. Back flick 10
7. Flick back 11
8. Toe to toe 12
9. Double decker 13
32. Beanstalk 36
49. Smuggle 53
50. Recruit 54

---

50 Brilliant PE Challenges Using Just a Beanbag

Lightning Source UK Ltd.
Milton Keynes UK
UKOW06f0238070716

277788UK00001B/85/P